BBC earth

DO YOU KNOW?

Level 3

ANIMAL SENSES

Inspired by BBC Earth TV series and developed with input from BBC Earth natural history specialists

Written by Sarah Wassner-Flynn

Text adapted by Carrie Lewis

Series Editor: Nick Coates

LADYBIRD BOOKS

UK | USA | Canada | Ireland | Australia
India | New Zealand | South Africa

Ladybird Books is part of the Penguin Random House group of companies
whose addresses can be found at global.penguinrandomhouse.com.
www.penguin.co.uk   www.puffin.co.uk   www.ladybird.co.uk

First published 2020
001

Printed in China

A CIP catalogue record for this book is available from the British Library

ISBN: 978-0-241-35577-0

All correspondence to:
Ladybird Books Ltd
Penguin Random House Children's
One Embassy Gardens, New Union Square
5 Nine Elms Lane, London SW8 5DA

Contents

New words

hearing

insect

lay eggs

nectar

predator

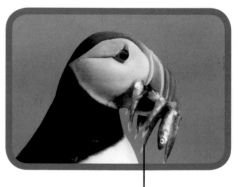

prey
(noun)

sight

smell
(noun and verb)

sound

tongue

touch
(noun and verb)

whisker

What are senses?

People have five senses. We use our eyes to see (**sight**), our ears to hear (**hearing**) and our noses to **smell**. We use our hands to **touch** and our **tongues** to taste.

Animals have senses, too.

A bald eagle has very good sight.

Animals use their senses to find food and to stay safe from **predators**.

A hunting dog can hear very well.

A butterfly tastes its food with its feet.

An octopus uses its suckers to touch things.

sucker

 PROJECT

Work in a group.
Make a chart about the five senses: sight, hearing, smell, touch and taste. What things do you see, hear, smell, touch or taste in a day? Write down everything you can think of.

Which animals can see in the dark?

Some animals can see things in the dark!

Leopards can see at night when it is very dark.

Some animals sleep in the day and go out at night. They are called nocturnal animals.

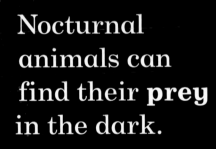

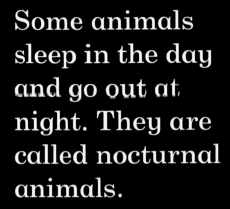

Nocturnal animals can find their **prey** in the dark.

This barn owl is looking for its prey.

📖 **FIND OUT!**

Use books or the internet to find one more animal that is nocturnal. What senses does it have that help it at night?

Which animals cannot see very well?

Some animals do not have very good sight. They must use different senses.

A naked mole rat cannot see very well.

Moles have small eyes and do not see very well. They use touch and smell to find prey and to stay safe.

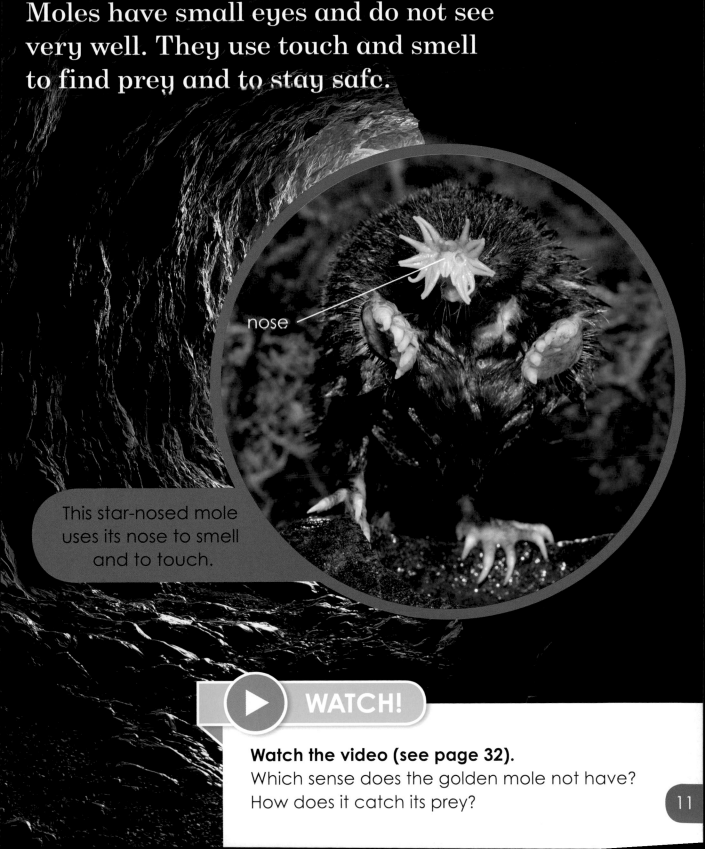

nose

This star-nosed mole uses its nose to smell and to touch.

▶ WATCH!

Watch the video (see page 32).
Which sense does the golden mole not have?
How does it catch its prey?

Which
animals can
hear well?

Many animals use their hearing to stay safe from predators.

Some animals, like dogs, can hear **sounds** that people cannot hear.

Dogs can move their ears to hear different sounds.

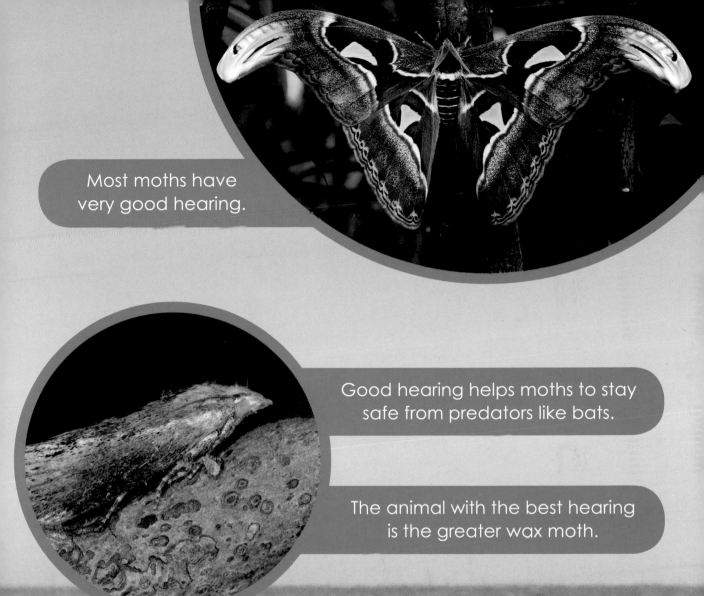

Most moths have very good hearing.

Good hearing helps moths to stay safe from predators like bats.

The animal with the best hearing is the greater wax moth.

FIND OUT!

Use books or the internet to find out how moths hear. Do they have ears?

Which animal uses its legs to listen?

People use their ears to hear but crickets are different. Crickets can hear with their legs! They have very good hearing.

Crickets have little ears on their legs.

Other **insects**, like katydids, also hear with their legs.

Elephants are big animals with very good senses. They use their feet to feel when other elephants move.

THINK!

What do elephants have that help them to hear things?

How do dolphins use sound?

Dolphins use echolocation to hear.

A dolphin makes sounds when it swims.
The sounds hit things in the water
like sand, fish and other dolphins.

Then, the sounds come back to
the dolphin. This is called an echo.
The dolphin understands
the echo and knows
where things are.

Dolphins make sounds all the time.

All dolphins use echolocation. It helps them to stay safe and to find food.

FIND OUT!

Use books or the internet to find out if any other animals use echolocation.

Which animals have the best sense of smell?

A shark's sense of smell is much better than a person's sense of smell.

Sharks use smell to find other animals. It helps them to find prey in the water.

A shark is a very good predator because it has a good sense of smell.

nare

Sharks smell with their nares. The nares are close to the shark's mouth.

THINK!

What other parts of a shark's body help it to find prey in the water?

Bears have a very good sense of smell.

They use their noses to find food from far away.

This polar bear is looking for a seal. It can smell the seal before it can see it.

A black bear can smell food from many kilometres away.

WATCH!

Watch the video (see page 32).
Which sense does the polar bear use to find the seal?
What other senses does it use?

How does a snake smell?

Snakes have a nose, but they don't use it like we do.

Snakes also use their tongues to 'taste' a smell.

This racer snake is using its sense of smell to understand what is near.

Smells help the snake to understand where it is and what is near.

Sea snakes live in the water. They use sight and smell to find their food.

LOOK!

Look at the pages.
What is interesting about the shape of a snake's tongue?

Which animals taste with their feet?

Butterflies walk on their feet and they can taste with them, too!

Butterflies walk on flowers and taste the **nectar**.

They taste leaves with their feet when they want to **lay eggs**.

This butterfly is tasting the leaf with its feet.

The butterfly is choosing a good leaf to lay its eggs on.

When the caterpillars come out of the eggs, they eat the leaves.

The right leaf is good food for caterpillars.

THINK!

Would you like to taste things with your feet? Why? Why not?

Which animal has the **most taste** buds?

Most animals have taste buds.

Our taste buds are on our tongues. They tell us about our food.

Earthworms have taste buds all over their bodies.

A catfish can find food in dark water.

It has taste buds all over its body.

These taste buds help the catfish to taste food when it swims.

PROJECT

Work in a group.
Talk about your favourite foods and make a chart showing whether these foods are sweet, salty, bitter or sour. Which flavour is the most popular?

How do whiskers help animals to touch?

Some animals use touch to understand where they are.

Whiskers help some animals to touch what is around them.

When the animal moves, the whiskers touch things.

Lions and all cats have whiskers.

Sea lions have very long whiskers.

Seals use their whiskers to hunt prey. Whiskers give seals a very good sense of touch.

▶ **WATCH!**

Watch the video (see page 32).
How do sea lions use their whiskers?

Quiz

Choose the correct answers.

1 Which of these animals cannot see well?

  a a leopard

  b an owl

  c a mole

2 Crickets can hear with their. . .

  a eyes.

  b legs.

  c heads.

3 Elephants feel movement with their . . .

  a feet.

  b tail.

  c ears.

4 Dolphins use echolocation. Echolocation works by using . . .

  a smell.

  b sound.

  c touch.

5 Sharks 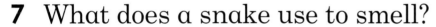 with their nares.
a hear
b see
c smell

6 What does a black bear
use to find prey?
a its nose
b its feet
c its ears

7 What does a snake use to smell?
a its eyes
b its tongue
c its feet

8 Whiskers help animals to . . .
a smell.
b touch.
c hear.

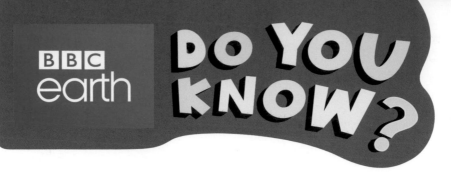

Visit www.ladybirdeducation.co.uk for FREE **DO YOU KNOW?** teaching resources.

- video clips with simplified voiceover and subtitles
- video and comprehension activities
- class projects and lesson plans
- audio recording of every book
- digital version of every book
- full answer keys

To access video clips, audio tracks and digital books:

1 Go to **www.ladybirdeducation.co.uk**
2 Click "Unlock book"
3 Enter the code below

t1bz0xCn5P

Stay safe online! Some of the DO YOU KNOW? activities ask children to do extra research online. Remember:

- ensure an adult is supervising;
- use established search engines such as Google or Kiddle;
- children should never share personal details, such as name, home or school address, telephone number or photos.